BELGICA

GAULISH VILLAGE

COMPENDIUM

LAUDANUM

AQUARIUM

TOTORUM

ARMORICA

·LUTETIA

SPQR

# GAUL
( ROMAN CONQUEST )
50 BC

CELTICA

AQUITANIA

PROVINCIA

THE YEAR IS 50 BC. GAUL IS ENTIRELY OCCUPIED BY THE
ROMANS. WELL, NOT ENTIRELY ... ONE SMALL VILLAGE OF
INDOMITABLE GAULS STILL HOLDS OUT AGAINST THE INVADERS.
AND LIFE IS NOT EASY FOR THE ROMAN LEGIONARIES WHO
GARRISON THE FORTIFIED CAMPS OF TOTORUM, AQUARIUM,
LAUDANUM AND COMPENDIUM ...

ASTERIX, THE HERO OF THESE ADVENTURES. A SHREWD, CUNNING LITTLE WARRIOR, ALL PERILOUS MISSIONS ARE IMMEDIATELY ENTRUSTED TO HIM. ASTERIX GETS HIS SUPERHUMAN STRENGTH FROM THE MAGIC POTION BREWED BY THE DRUID GETAFIX . . .

OBELIX, ASTERIX'S INSEPARABLE FRIEND. A MENHIR DELIVERY MAN BY TRADE, ADDICTED TO WILD BOAR. OBELIX IS ALWAYS READY TO DROP EVERYTHING AND GO OFF ON A NEW ADVENTURE WITH ASTERIX – SO LONG AS THERE'S WILD BOAR TO EAT, AND PLENTY OF FIGHTING. HIS CONSTANT COMPANION IS DOGMATIX, THE ONLY KNOWN CANINE ECOLOGIST, WHO HOWLS WITH DESPAIR WHEN A TREE IS CUT DOWN.

GETAFIX, THE VENERABLE VILLAGE DRUID, GATHERS MISTLETOE AND BREWS MAGIC POTIONS. HIS SPECIALITY IS THE POTION WHICH GIVES THE DRINKER SUPERHUMAN STRENGTH. BUT GETAFIX ALSO HAS OTHER RECIPES UP HIS SLEEVE . . .

CACOFONIX, THE BARD. OPINION IS DIVIDED AS TO HIS MUSICAL GIFTS. CACOFONIX THINKS HE'S A GENIUS. EVERY-ONE ELSE THINKS HE'S UNSPEAKABLE. BUT SO LONG AS HE DOESN'T SPEAK, LET ALONE SING, EVERYBODY LIKES HIM . . .

FINALLY, VITALSTATISTIX, THE CHIEF OF THE TRIBE. MAJESTIC, BRAVE AND HOT-TEMPERED, THE OLD WARRIOR IS RESPECTED BY HIS MEN AND FEARED BY HIS ENEMIES. VITALSTATISTIX HIMSELF HAS ONLY ONE FEAR, HE IS AFRAID THE SKY MAY FALL ON HIS HEAD TOMORROW. BUT AS HE ALWAYS SAYS, TOMORROW NEVER COMES.

GOSCINNY AND UDERZO
PRESENT
*An Asterix Adventure*

# ASTERIX
# AND THE
# CAULDRON

*Written by* RENÉ GOSCINNY *and Illustrated by* ALBERT UDERZO

*Translated by* Anthea Bell *and* Derek Hockridge

ORION

Revised edition and English translation © 2004 HACHETTE

Original title: *Astérix et le Chaudron*

Exclusive Licensee: Orion Publishing Group
Translators: Anthea Bell and Derek Hockridge
Typography: Bryony Newhouse

This revised edition first published in 2004 by
Orion Books Ltd
Orion House, 5 Upper St Martin's Lane
London WC2H 9EA

Printed in France by Partenaires

http://gb.asterix.com
www.orionbooks.co.uk

A CIP catalogue record for this book is available from the British Library

ISBN 0752866281 (cased)
ISBN 075286629X (paperback)

Distributed in the United States of America by Sterling Publishing Co. Inc.
387 Park Avenue South, New York, NY 10016

THE SPRINGTIME CALM OF THE LITTLE VILLAGE WE KNOW SO WELL IS INTERRUPTED BY THE ANNOUNCEMENT OF AN OFFICIAL VISIT...

IF YOU THINK I'D TAKE A PART IN ANY GLEE WITH YOU, FULLIAUTOMATIX...

ANY MORE SINGING AND YOU GET TAKEN APART! WITH GLEE!

CHIEF WHOSEMORALSARELASTIX AND HIS MEN ARE ON THEIR WAY!

STRAIGHT AWAY A COUNCIL MEETING IS CALLED.

WHO IS THIS CHIEF WHOSEMORALS- ARELASTIX?

HE'S THE CHIEF OF A VILLAGE ON THE CLIFF TOPS. I DON'T LIKE HIM MUCH; HE'S TIGHT-FISTED AND HE'LL DO ANY SORT OF DEAL WITH THE ROMANS FOR MONEY ...

HOWEVER, HE IS A GAULISH CHIEF! WHEN ONE GAULISH CHIEF MEETS ANOTHER GAULISH CHIEF, PROTOCOL MUST BE OBSERVED! LET PREPARATIONS BE MADE TO WELCOME HIM!

SOON AFTER- WARDS ...

NOW THEN, BOYS! DECORUM, DIGNITY, NOBILITY!

HERE HE COMES, CHIEF!

WOTCHER, MATE! BIT WARM, EH? HOW ABOUT A JAR?

?!?!

5

HAVE YOU COME ALL BY YOURSELF LIKE THAT?

OH, NO! HERE'S MY RETINUE.

?

WHAT THE... IT'S A CAULDRON!

YES, THAT'S WHY I HAD TO WALK. THERE'S NOT MUCH ROOM ON THESE SHIELDS.

YOU MEAN YOU GAVE UP YOUR SHIELD TO THIS CAULDRON? WHAT'S SO SPECIAL ABOUT IT?

IT'S FULL OF SESTERTII, BY TOUTATIS! COME OVER HERE ... I'VE GOT SOMETHING TO TELL YOU.

JULIUS CAESAR IS IN GRAVE FINANCIAL DIFFICULTIES. HE'S USED THE TAXES WHICH WERE GOING TO PAY HIS GARRISONS HERE IN GAUL TO EQUIP HIS ARMIES FOR NEW CAMPAIGNS ...

I HEARD THAT CAESAR WAS ABOUT TO LEVY NEW TAXES, SO I PUT ALL MY PEOPLE'S SAVINGS IN THIS CAULDRON, AND I'VE BROUGHT IT TO YOU FOR SAFE KEEPING ... I BELIEVE YOU DON'T PAY ANY TAXES?...

WELL, A TAX COLLECTOR DID SHOW UP ONE DAY ... WE HAVEN'T PAID ANY TAXES SINCE!

DEAR ME! ... I'LL NEVER FORGET HOW WE SHOWED HIM UP!

WHAT FUN WE HAD! REMEMBER WHEN ...?

OH, DO STOP! HOHOHO!

YOU MEAN HE NEVER RETURNED?

THAT'S RIGHT. NO RETURN, NO TAX RETURN, NO TAXES!

WHEN I KNEW WHAT THE ROMANS INTENDED TO DO I DIDN'T HESITATE! I GRABBED THE FIRST AVAILABLE CONTAINER, THREW OUT THE ONION SOUP SIMMERING INSIDE IT, AND FILLED IT WITH ALL MY SESTERTII.

AND I HAVE BROUGHT IT TO YOU FOR SAFE KEEPING! THE ROMANS WILL NEVER DARE TO LOOK FOR IT HERE!

BUT COULDN'T YOU HAVE HIDDEN THE MONEY ... BURIED IT?

NO. THE ROMANS ARE ALWAYS EXCAVATING ... THERE ARE SO MANY BURIED TAXES ABOUT THEY'LL PROBABLY BE GETTING DUG UP FOR CENTURIES TO COME!

IT'S A GOOD IDEA TO PREVENT THE ROMANS GETTING THEIR HANDS ON THIS MONEY ...

IT IS, ISN'T IT?

...BUT I THOUGHT YOU WERE IN THEIR GOOD TABLETS ... ESPECIALLY AS THE ROMANS LIKE PEOPLE WHO PAY THEIR TAXES REGULARLY.

WHAT?

YOU'VE NO RIGHT TO DOUBT MY PATRIOTISM! I MAY DO BUSINESS WITH THE ROMANS ...

...BUT I ALWAYS MAKE THEM PAY TWICE THE PRICE I'D HAVE CHARGED MY GAULISH CUSTOMERS!

THAT'S GOOD!

VERY GOOD!

AND DO YOU DO MUCH BUSINESS WITH GAULS?

NO ... THE ROMANS BUY EVERYTHING I'VE GOT TO SELL!

VERY WELL, WE'LL LOOK AFTER YOUR CAULDRON UNTIL THE TAX COLLECTOR HAS BEEN.

I WILL PUT IT IN THE HANDS OF MY MOST TRUSTWORTHY WARRIOR: ASTERIX!

I'M GOING TO PUT THE CAULDRON IN MY HUT.

HOW SILLY! FANCY THROWING OUT GOOD ONION SOUP TO MAKE ROOM FOR SESTERTII!

BUT OBELIX, WITH SESTERTII YOU CAN BUY ONION SOUP!

THAT'S THE POINT! WHY THROW OUT THE ONION SOUP WHEN IT WAS IN THE CAULDRON ALREADY?

I WILL STAND GUARD ALL NIGHT.

ER ... THERE'S GOING TO BE A BANQUET FOR CHIEF WHOSEMORALS-ARELASTIX. I DON'T LIKE TO DEPRIVE DOGMATIX OF ...

OFF YOU GO, OBELIX, OLD CHAP!

I'LL BRING YOU SOMETHING TO EAT!

WOOF! WOOF!

SOON AFTERWARDS...

YUM! SCRUNCH! GLOUP!

BY TOUTATIS! YOU EAT WELL!

EAT? ... GLOUP! ...

EAT? I'D FORGOTTEN ALL ABOUT ASTERIX! I MUST TAKE HIM SOMETHING TO EAT!

YOU JUST SIT STILL! I'LL SEE TO IT! I'VE GOT A BIT OF INFORMATION TO GIVE HIM.

YOU'RE WELCOME ... SCRUNCH! ... I HATE BREAKING OFF BETWEEN TWO ... YUM! ... BOARS!

10

11

16

19

PALACE OF THE GLADIATORS

WHO'S FIRST?

LUCKY BLIGHTER! HE'S SURE TO GET THE PRIZE!

NEXT!

AND NEXT COMES THE NEXT...

AND THE NEXT!

...AND RUNNING PRACTICALLY NECK AND NECK, THE NEXT...

AND THE NEXT!

AND THE NEXT!

AND THE NEXT!

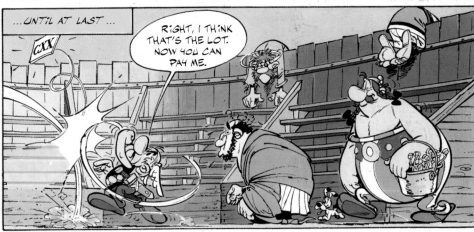

...UNTIL AT LAST...

RIGHT, I THINK THAT'S THE LOT. NOW YOU CAN PAY ME.

WHAT DO YOU MEAN, PAY YOU? YOUR FAT FRIEND DID IN ALL MY GLADIATORS, YOU'VE DONE IN MY ENTIRE AUDIENCE, YOU'VE GONE AND RUINED ME AND YOU WANT TO GET PAID AS WELL?

TAP! TAP! TAP! TAP!

YOU JUST GIVE ME BACK MY MAGNIFICENT WORKS OF ART!

WHAT FAT FRIEND?

OH, GIVE HIM HIS STATUETTES, OBELIX.

23

WHAT'S THAT?

A MODERN THEATRE. THE ROMANS ARE BUILDING THEM ALL OVER THE PLACE: ARAUSIO,* ARELATUM,** VIENNA.***

* ORANGE
** ARLES
*** VIENNE

YOU, SIR, ARE A BARBARIAN! A PHILISTINE!

LET ME TELL YOU, SIR, I HAVE PERFORMED AT ROME, BEFORE JULIUS CAESAR HIMSELF!

I'VE TOURED ALEXANDRIA! QUEEN CLEOPATRA THREW A PARTY FOR ME!

I GOT A STANDING OVATION AT MASSILIA!

YOUR NOTIONS OF THE THEATRE ARE LITERALLY ANTIQUATED! ARISTOPHANES, PLAUTUS, TERENCE ... THEY'RE ALL ON THE SHELF! THEY'VE HAD TO MAKE WAY FOR THE NEW DRAMA, WHICH HAS SOMETHING TO SAY!

WELL, I'VE GOT SOMETHING TO SAY ALL RIGHT!

DON'T LOWER YOURSELF, DEAR BOY! LET'S GO!

WE'LL SEE HOW THAT YOUNG FELLOW GETS ON WITHOUT US!

I CAN REPLACE YOU BY THE NEXT TWO IDIOTS WHO COME MY WAY, AND WHAT'S MORE, I'LL GAIN ON THE DEAL!

HEY! YOU THERE! YOU TWO EVER DONE ANY ACTING?

WHAT, US? NO.

LIKE TO HAVE A GO?

DOES IT PAY?

HM ... I SEE YOU NEVER HAVE DONE ANY ACTING ... EXCELLENT! YOU WILL IMPORT A NEW ELEMENT ... A BREATH OF FRESH AIR! THE VITAL THING IS, YOU MUST HAVE SOMETHING TO SAY.

PERSONALLY I'VE GOT A CAULDRON TO FILL.

MARVELLOUS! GREAT! WHAT A LINE! YOU'LL MAKE THEATRICAL HISTORY. COME WITH ME! YOU'VE GOT TALENT!

?

?

24

THE SHOW STARTS...

'DING! DONG!

WHAT AN UGLY LOT YOU ARE! WE MAY BE UGLY TOO, BUT YOU'RE WORSE!

YAAAH!

IT'S SO DREADFULLY AUTHENTIC...!

ORGIES! ORGIES! WE WANT ORGIES!

STOP! STOP! THIS IS DISGRACEFUL! THEY'RE MAKING FUN OF US!

HE'S RIGHT!

NO, HE ISN'T!

THROW HIM OUT!

MUSEUM PIECES!

ROMAN RELICS!

THAT'S YOUR CUE! GO ON! GO ON, THEN!

I ...I'LL NEVER MAKE IT!

THINK OF THE CAULDRON!

32

NEXT DAY, STILL AT CONDATUM, AND...

STILL NOT A SESTERTIUS!

WE COULD SELL THE CAULDRON?

HOW WOULD THAT HELP TO FILL IT?

I SHALL NEVER, NEVER BE ABLE TO GO HOME TO OUR VILLAGE AGAIN!

THERE, THERE, ASTERIX! I'M SURE TOUTATIS WILL HELP US!

?!?

DING! TING!

DONG!

I HATE TO SEE PEOPLE LOOKING SAD WHEN I'M SO HAPPY! I'VE JUST WON A PACKET.

DING! DING! DING!

DING! DING!

?!?!

HEY! WON IT? WON IT HOW?

AT THE RACES, MATE! AT THE RACES!

TING!

I ONLY HAD A FEW SESTERTII, I PUT THEM ON A CHARIOT, AND I WON!

WHERE EXACTLY ARE THE RACES?

IN THE HIPPODROME. FOLLOW ME; I'M GOING BACK TO MAKE ANOTHER PILE.

THERE, ASTERIX, WHAT DID I SAY?

THAT'S THE HIPPODROME. WELL, GOODBYE AND GOOD LUCK.

YOU KNOW, WHEN WE DO HAVE A BIT OF CASH FOR ONCE, I HATE TO RISK IT!

BUT THERE'S NO RISK! WE PLACE OUR BET AND WE FILL THE CAULDRON! THAT'S WHAT HE SAID.

33

* CHARIOTEER

30A

30B

34

HARD LUCK, FRIENDS! BUT MY BROTHER-IN-LAW HAPPENS TO KNOW THE NEPHEW OF THE AURIGA OF THE GREEN CHARIOT IN THE NEXT RACE, AND HE...

WE HAVEN'T GOT ANY MORE MONEY! AND YOU TOLD ME IT WAS IMPOSSIBLE FOR THE BLUE CHARIOT TO LOSE!

IMPOSSIBLE IS NOT A GAULISH WORD, MY FRIENDS!

!

(SIGH) (SIGH) (SIGH)

(SIGH)

COME ON, OBELIX. I'VE STILL GOT A FEW BRONZE COINS LEFT. LET'S HAVE A BITE TO EAT.

SOON AFTERWARDS...

I RECOMMEND THE BOAR; IT'S VERY GOOD VALUE JUST NOW. PRICES HAVE FALLEN; BOAR ARE BEING SOLD FIFTEEN TO THE DOZEN AT THE MOMENT.

BARCLVS BANK

?

WHAT'S THAT? A TEMPLE?

NEAR ENOUGH. IT'S A ROMAN BANK. WHERE THEY KEEP THEIR GOLD.

YOU KNOW WHAT WE'RE GOING TO DO?

EAT OUR BOARS?

NO! WE ARE GOING TO ROB THAT BANK! THE ROMANS TAKE OUR MONEY, SO IT'S NO CRIME TO TAKE IT BACK FROM THEM!

BUT HOW DO YOU ROB A BANK?

I HAVE A PLAN ... LANDLORD!

OLACK...

CAN YOU LET US HAVE A ROOM WITH A VIEW OF THE BANK?

A VIEW OF THE BANK?

SCRUNCH! SCRUNCH!

WELL, HAVE YOU GOT A ROOM WITH A VIEW OF THE SEA?

WHAT, IN CONDATUM? OF COURSE NOT!

RIGHT, ONE WITH A VIEW OF THE BANK, THEN!

THAT SEEMS LOGICAL ... FOLLOW ME.

SOON AFTERWARDS ...

FINE. I'M OFF TO DO A BIT OF SHOPPING. MEANWHILE, I WANT YOU TO LOITER AROUND THE BANK, LOOKING INNOCENT. YOU MUST TRY AND FIND OUT WHAT TIME THE GUARD CHANGES, AND WHERE THEY KEEP THE GOLD.

SCRUNCH! SCRUNCH!

SCRUNCH! SCRUNCH!

LOOK INNOCENT? HOW DO I DO THAT?

HOW SHOULD I KNOW? YOU'RE SUPPOSED TO HAVE ALL THIS TALENT FOR ACTING ... YOU CAN STROLL BY, WHISTLING NONCHALANTLY!

TRUE ... I FORGOT MY TALENT FOR ACTING ... LET'S GO!

WE'LL MEET BACK AT THE INN. BE CAREFUL.

THERE WE ARE, OBELIX! I'VE WORKED OUT THE TIMES THEY CHANGE GUARD!

I NOTICE THAT ABOUT ELEVEN IN THE MORNING THE SENTRY LEAVES HIS POST TO HAVE A DRINK OF WATER AT THE FOUNTAIN...

THAT'S OUR MOMENT TO ACT.

YAAAAWN!

LOOK, I'VE DRAWN UP A PLAN.

SCRATCH! SCRATCH!

SCRATCH! SCRATCH!

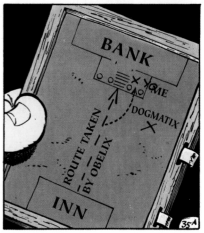

BANK

DOGMATIX X

ROUTE TAKEN BY OBELIX

INN

35-A

DOGMATIX WILL KEEP WATCH AND WARN US IF THE SENTRY COMES BACK SOONER THAN EXPECTED... YOU BREAK DOWN THE DOOR...

I'M HIDING BEHIND THE THIRD COLUMN. I LEAP IN...

WE SHALL HAVE FIVE MINUTES TO CARRY OUT THE OPERATION BEFORE THE SENTRY GETS BACK. DURING THIS TIME, WE HAVE TO QUESTION THE STAFF AND FIND THE GOLD... GET IT?

NO.

RIGHT. NEVER MIND. WE PLOUGH INTO THEM, WE PICK UP THE CASH, AND WE BEAT IT.

I GET THAT!

TOiiiNG!

GLUG. GLUG. GLUG. GLUG.

35-B

THIS DOOR WILL NEVER STAND UP TO THE MAGIC POTION...

BANG!

OH!

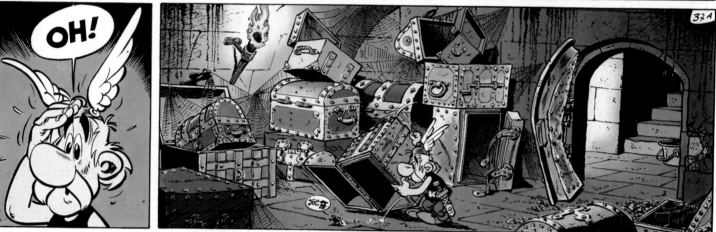

HEY, WHAT ARE YOU DOING HERE? IF YOU WANT TO DEPOSIT MONEY, YOU HAVE TO DO IT AT THE COUNTER UPSTAIRS.

I DIDN'T COME TO DEPOSIT MONEY, I CAME TO TAKE SOME.

BANG!

OH, I THOUGHT IT WAS A BIT STRANGE!

BUT WE DON'T HAVE ANY MONEY LEFT, MY POOR FELLOW! NOT A SESTERTIUS! THAT'S WHY CAESAR LEVIES TAXES ... QUID PRO QUO, OLD CHAP. AT LEAST, PLENTY OF QUID PRO CAESAR, BUT PRECIOUS LITTLE FOR ANYONE ELSE, OH, CAESAR'S A REAL OLD PRO!

COME ALONG, OBELIX!

AND STOP THAT WHISTLING!

OK.

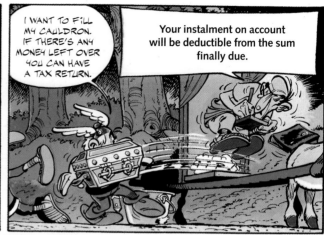

O CHIEF WHOSEMORALS-ARELASTIX! HERE'S THE MONEY!

MONEY? WHERE? WHERE?

OH... IT'S YOU!

I AM RETURNING THE SESTERTII YOU ENTRUSTED TO MY CARE ... I RATHER THINK THE TAX COLLECTOR HAS ALREADY CALLED?

THAT'S RIGHT... HE DIDN'T FIND ANY MONEY HERE, SO HE LEFT ... WELL, THANKS VERY MUCH ...

JUST A MOMENT!

?!

HOWEVER, THE CHIEF IS WRONG! HIS SESTERTII ARE NOT LOST TO THE ENTIRE HUMAN RACE... AT THE VERY MOMENT WHEN THE CAULDRON FALLS, A PIRATE SHIP IS SAILING PAST THE CLIFF...

CHLONK!

MUTINY! SUFFERING SEASERPENTS, WHO DARED CROWN ME WITH A CAULDRON?

AND FOR ONCE, JUST FOR ONCE, THE PIRATES ARE HAPPY!

ONION-FLAVOURED, TOO! MY FAVOURITE KIND!

SESTERTII FROM OLYMPUS! THIS SHOULD KEEP OUR HEADS ABOVE WATER!

AS HAPPY AS OUR FRIENDS, THE TOAST OF THE WHOLE VILLAGE, WHICH, THANKS TO THEM, HAS PRESERVED ITS HONOUR INTACT!

BUT WHAT I NEVER DID UNDERSTAND IS WHY ANYONE WOULD PUT MONEY IN THAT CAULDRON INSTEAD OF ONION SOUP IN THE FIRST PLACE!

THE END

UDERZO & GOSCINNY